When You Lick a Slug, Your Tongue Goes Numb

Kids Share Their Wit and Wisdom

with

H. Jackson Brown, Jr.

RUTLEDGE HILL PRESS
Nashville, Tennessee

Previously published in hardcover as *Wit and Wisdom from the Peanut Butter Gang.*

Published in Nashville, Tennessee, by Rutledge Hill Press, Inc., 211 Seventh Avenue North, Nashville, Tennessee 37219. Distributed in Canada by H. B. Fenn and Company Ltd., Mississauga, Ontario. Designed by Ellis Design

Library of Congress Cataloging-in-Publication Data

When you lick a slug, your tongue goes numb / compiled and edited by
   H. Jackson Brown, Jr.
    p.   cm.
   ISBN 1-55853-326-5
   1. Children—Quotations. I. Brown, H. Jackson, 1940-   .
PN6328.C5W47 1995
305.23—dc20   95-2626
                                     CIP

Printed in the United States of America
1 2 3 4 5 6 7 8 9 — 98 97 96 95

CONTENTS

Dedicated to
the child-like spirit
that lives in every heart–
both young and old.

introduction

"IF I WANT TO KNOW HOW MY NEW HAIRSTYLE REALLY LOOKS, I ask the five-year-old who lives next door." My aunt made this comment several years ago, and I've never forgotten it. Children have an uncanny ability to discover and deliver the truth, and we're often caught off guard by their insight, imagination, and truth-piercing humor.

I'm reminded of this every day when I read my morning mail. Among the letters are always notes from youngsters. It's easy to guess the age of my correspondent. If the address on the envelope is slanted more than ten degrees, he or she is under ten—less than ten degrees, ten or over. Often when I open the envelopes, sparkling confetti or a class picture comes tumbling out. I never know quite what to expect, but I am always touched by the innocence and perceptiveness of the children who write to me. These letters confirmed my belief that the special visions of young people deserve special attention.

Funny and smart, poignant and wise, sentimental and sassy, young people remind us that we're never too old to learn or too young to teach. The observations of these children and their colorful artwork tug at our hearts, lift our spirits, and reacquaint us with our own lost childhood—a time when we eagerly approached each day with excitement, confidence, and wonder.

Other books by H. Jackson Brown, Jr.

A Father's Book of Wisdom
P.S. I Love You
Life's Little Instruction Book
Live and Learn and Pass It On
Life's Little Instruction Book, Volume II
Live and Learn and Pass It On, Volume II
Life's Little Treasure Book on Joy
Life's Little Treasure Book on Marriage and Family
Life's Little Treasure Book on Wisdom
Life's Little Treasure Book on Success
Life's Little Treasure Book on Love
Life's Little Treasure Book on Parenting
The Little Book of Christmas Joys
(with Rosemary Brown and Kathy Peel)

Family

"IF LOVE ISN'T TAUGHT IN THE HOME, it is almost impossible to learn it anywhere else." In one sentence a seventy-five-year-old great-grandmother explained to me the importance of home and family.

The characteristics of the modern family have changed. Divorce and remarriage are more common. More mothers are employed outside the home, resulting in fathers playing a greater role in child rearing. There is an increase in one-parent families and stepfamilies, and statistics show that families are smaller and move more often. But children remind us that, in spite of the new dynamics of the family, some things remain the same. Moms and dads still surprise kids with their knowledge, confirming Mark Twain's observation that parents seem to get smarter as their children grow into adults. There's the special bond between children and their grandparents. And little brothers still drive sisters crazy (but big brothers with driver's licenses are another matter entirely).

The family defines our past and shapes our character. It is here that we learn the important lessons of self-discipline, the art of compromise, forgiveness, honesty, and fair play. And it's here that we learn why you shouldn't make faces behind your father's back—he'll catch you every time!

When your mother tells you that you will not like the out-come of your new experimental hair style, you should always listen. She knows what she's talking about.

— Rebecca, Age 15

You shouldn't listen in on your sister's conversation with her boyfriend because it gets too mushy.

— *Lezlee, Age 11*

When your mother is mad and asks you, "Do I look stupid?" it's best not to answer her.

— *Meghann, Age 13*

Sisters make great best friends.

— *Kellie, Age 13*

I'll never take my mom's car out again until I can do it legally.

— *Lorie, Age 14*

Parents freak out when you have a party with loud music.

— *Eddie, Age 10*

FAMILY

You can learn many things from children. How much patience you have, for instance.

— *Franklin P. Jones*

Every time my grandparents sleep over, they snore through the night.

— Megan, Age 6

If you want something expensive, you should ask your grandparents.

— Matthew, Age 12

You shouldn't stand in a bucket of water and touch an electric fence just because your brother tells you to.

— Melissa, Age 13

When I want to watch a TV show with my parents past my bedtime, my mom always sends me to bed no matter how much I fake being "absorbed" in the program.

— Rebecca, Age 11

Parents don't get enough appreciation.

— *Susanna, Age 17*

You should never laugh at your dad if he's mad or screaming at you.

— *John, Age 12*

My little brother's dirty diapers are worse than liver.

— *Matt, Age 11*

My parents won't go to sleep until I get home.

— *Abby, Age 16*

If mom's not happy, nobody's happy.

— *Neely, Age 13*

FAMILY

Children have never been very good at listening to their elders, but they have never failed to imitate them.

— *James Baldwin*

If your mom's asleep, don't wake her up.

— Amber, Age 10

You can play the coolest tricks when people don't know that you have a twin.

— *Amie, Age 16*

When my dad says to be home at 11:30, he doesn't mean be in the driveway, but inside the house by myself.

— *Elizabeth, Age 16*

If your mom picks your clothes and you dislike them, tell her they don't fit.

— *Christie, Age 12*

You only have one mom, and you should take care of her.

— *Sean, Age 12*

FAMILY

One of the luckiest things that can happen to you in life is, I think, to have a happy childhood.

— *Agatha Christie*

Every time I am at home and I am getting on my parents' nerves, they wish I were at camp. And every time I'm at camp and nothing's bothering them, they miss me.

— *Ashley, Age 12*

My grandmother can say more in a sentence than a college professor can say in an hour and a half.

— *Angela, Age 14*

No matter how much I love something, mom will throw it away without a second's thought.

— *Brian, Age 12*

My dad will never be color coordinated.

— *Samuel, Age 11*

When you complain about doing the dishes, you usually get stuck doing them more often.

— *Nichole, Age 14*

The older you get, the harder your parents try to keep you little.

— *Emily, Age 16*

Even today, watching baseball with your grandpa is still a great American pastime.

— *Erin, Age 13*

You should never pick on your sister when she has a baseball bat in her hands.

— *Joel, Age 12*

I can remember what flavor of ice cream cone my grandmother and I shared at Disneyworld; but, most of the time, I can't remember what day it is. I guess it depends on what you think is important.

— *Katherine, Age 13*

If you put your brother's hand in warm water, he *will* wet the bed.

— *Christopher, Age 9*

When you make a face behind your father's back, he turns around too quick for you to get away with it.

— *Elizabeth, Age 12*

It's no fun to stay up all night if your parents don't care.

— *Carrie, Age 15*

FAMILY

Why do grandparents and grandchildren get along so well? They have the same enemy— the mother.

— *Claudette Colbert*

You should never ask your three-year-old brother to hold a tomato.

— *Alecia, Age 12*

Every time I complain to my mom that I'm bored, she tells me to go clean my room.

— *Joanna, Age 13*

If your sister hits you, don't hit her back. Parents always catch the second person.

— *Michael, Age 10*

FAMILY

There's only one pretty child in the world, and every mother has it.

— *J. C. Bridge*

If mom says "no," she means it. If dad says "no," it means maybe.

— *Joseph, Age 13*

When I think about my grandpas who are dead, tears jump into my eyes.

— *Calen, Age 7*

Brothers are annoying until they get a car.

— *Leslie, Age 12*

No matter what I do, my mom can always tell when I'm lying.

— *Jamie, Age 16*

You have to be very sneaky if you borrow your sister's clothes without permission.

— *Emily Ann, Age 15*

It isn't the best thing to dump a bowl of ice cream over your brother's head —no matter how mad you are.

— *Laura, Age 12*

You can't play sick and then expect your mom to let you go to the mall after school.

— *Wendy, Age 14*

When your mom is mad at your dad, don't let her brush your hair.

— *Morgan, Age 11*

Once you've lost your parents' trust, it's hard to earn it back.

— *Kara, Age 13*

Even when freshly washed and relieved of all obvious confections, children tend to be sticky.

— *Fran Lebowitz*

Oh, to be only half as wonderful as my child thought I was when he was small, and only half as stupid as my teenager now thinks I am.

— Rebecca Richards

You should not pick your nose because your mom will SCREAM!!!

— Tiffany, Age 8

If you live with five other women, you have to get up bright and early to get into the bathroom.

— Meghann, Age 13

One of the greatest feelings in the world is the feeling you get when your little sister shows that she admires you.

— Dawn, Age 14

I appreciate my mom more than she knows.

— David, Age 15

Parents have eyes in the backs of their heads.

— *Melissa, Age 12*

You shouldn't bug a pregnant mom.

— *Nicholas, Age 11*

Despite all the loving and caring relationships in the world, there is nothing more loving than the feel of my mother's hand on my forehead when I am sick.

— Rosemary, Age 17

It seems like the oldest one always gets in trouble even if she didn't do it.

— Sally, Age 11

When you bring a date to your house, dodge your parents.

— Brian, Age 17

Parents should come with instructions.

— Shanna, Age 14

FAMILY

Before I got married, I had six theories about bringing up children; now, I have six children and no theories.

— John Wilmont, Earl of Rochester

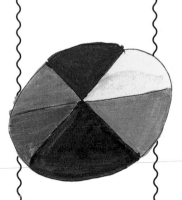

It's not always easy being a kid, but I bet it's even harder being an adult.

— *Julie, Age 11*

I shouldn't ask my dad what a word means unless I want to look it up in the dictionary.

— *Angela, Age 9*

You should never tell your parents when you're curious and want to ask a question about girls because many lectures will come in the future.

— *Reza, Age 12*

Friends

I WAS LUCKY. I HAD A HAPPY CHILDHOOD, and I carry it in my pocket like a gold coin. Sam was the main reason. He was my best friend and lived across the street. After fifty years, I still remember his telephone number: 8-7968. We were inseparable for the first twelve years of our lives. Sam was funny, smart, and best of all he could keep secrets. He also had a pony with a real leather saddle and a huge swing set the size of those you see in park playgrounds.

We formed a secret club that met every afternoon at two o'clock. We had a secret sign, a secret motto, and a secret handshake.

Sam and I still live in the same city, and a couple of weeks ago we got together for lunch. As we were leaving we gave each other the secret handshake, the secret sign, and the secret motto that ends with three Indian-like war-whoops. The restaurant was crowded, but we didn't care, happily proving Ralph Waldo Emerson's observation that, "It is the blessing of old friends that you can be stupid with them."

Children know the value of making and keeping friends. They have discovered that being a friend takes work and that a good friend can sometimes be the person you least expected to care about you. They will tell you that friends sometimes let you down and that nothing hurts as much as watching a good friend move away.

And they will admit that even an old guy like Emerson knew a thing or two when he said, "The only way to have a friend is to be one."

FRIENDS

Oh, to hear the whispers between two children.

Being a good friend is a twenty-four-hour job.

— *Jill, Age 14*

When you are sick, friends can sometimes be a better medicine than the kind the doctor gives you.

— *Julie Anne, Age 12*

You should never tell your friends your parents' nickname for you or you'll never hear the end of it.

— *Jennifer, Age 12*

If you tell your friend that you like a boy and say that she can tell only one person, she tells the world.

— *Melissa, Age 13*

When you
buy a car for
the first time,
your number of
friends increases
dramatically.

— *Jeffrey, Age 16*

When you move, you find out who your true friends are by the ones who make an effort to keep in touch with you.

— Kelly, Age 11

No matter how many friends you have, there is always room for one more.

— Andrea, Age 14

My REAL friends aren't the ones I go out with, but the ones who listen to me when I need an ear and the ones I can cry to when I need a shoulder.

— Cory, Age 17

Your best friends are the ones who don't believe the rumors about you.

— Maria, Age 13

You never put a boyfriend before family. Family will always be there— boyfriends come and go.

— Jessica, Age 16

God gives us our relatives; thank God we can choose our friends.

— *Ethel Wats Mumford*

You should not be the first one to fall asleep at a slumber party.

— *Katie, Age 12*

If you have true friends, you can get through anything.

— *Jessica, Age 15*

If you give your enemy a second chance, she might turn out to be your best friend.

— *Meghann, Age 13*

Old friends are like old sneakers— always comfortable.

— *Lindsay, Age 12.*

FRIENDS

There is in friendship something of all relations, and something above them all. It is the gold thread that ties the heart of all the world.

— *John Evelyn*

FRIENDS

**Instead of loving
your enemies,
treat your friends
a little better.**

— Ed Howe

One best friend is better than a whole bunch of friends.

— Kim, Age 11

Having a friend that you can confide in is better than a million dollars.

— Rachel, Age 12

My true friends are those who are there for me, not just to cheer me up, but to cheer me on.

— Elise, Age 14

Real true friends are the ones who don't mind driving ten miles out of their way to pick you up for school each morning.

— Donna, Age 17

You should never wear a red shirt with black polka dots because your friends will call you a lady bug.

— *Stefanie, Age 8*

You don't miss the old neighborhood until you move away.

— Melissa, Age 15

When my best friend moved away, it was only then that I realized just how special she is to me.

— Kate, Age 12

If you can't trust a friend, then that person really isn't your friend. What is a friend without trust?

— Andrea, Age 14

Everything is more fun with a friend.

— Rebekah, Age 15

School

THE CLASSROOM IS SECOND ONLY TO THE HOME in the important tasks of teaching young people cooperation, developing good moral habits, conveying a sense of responsibility, and instilling a love of learning. Good schools succeed at this and, almost without exception, they have three things in common: (1) caring, well-trained teachers, (2) courageous principals who let the teachers teach, and (3) parents and communities that get involved with school programs and activities.

It's hard to overestimate the influence a good teacher has on the development of a child. A friend, Carol Swaim, has told me, "Good teachers don't just teach lessons; they have lessons to teach." Our best teachers should be rewarded, honored, and cherished, and we need to do all we can to ensure that good teachers are well paid. What does it say about our priorities when the least successful professional athletes make more money than our best teachers?

Children know a good teacher when they see one. They might cause a slight disturbance in class now and then and may sometimes feign a stomachache to stay home on a test day, but they know that school is important and that good teachers deserve respect and attention. They have discovered that a wise teacher makes learning a joy.

I was a fantastic student until ten, and then my mind began to wander.

— Grace Paley

Reading what people write on desks can teach you a lot.

— Tiffany, Age 13

The class in school I hate the most is the one I learn the most from.

— Joanne, Age 10

The boys' restroom smells, but the girls' restroom doesn't.

— Devin, Age 10

All the bad things I've heard about algebra are true.

— Erin, Age 14

If you read a book, it can take you to places you haven't been before.

— Lindsay Ellen, Age 10

You can't catch a hard baseball in your mouth.

— Joseph, Age 10

When You Lick A Slug, Your Tongue Goes Numb

If you put a frog in a girl's desk, you're going to hear some screaming.

— *Nicholas, Age 9*

Making a good grade on a test you studied really hard for is a glorious feeling.

— Sarah, Age 12

When I am working in class and the teacher is looking over my shoulder, I get nervous.

— Tina, Age 17

When I try to be nice to my teachers because I think they deserve some respect, my friends always think I'm kissing up.

— Dawn, Age 14

If I do my homework on the bus, my mom never believes it.

— Adam, Age 9

When teachers get old, like over fifty-five, they're always in a bad mood.

— *Lindsey, Age 8*

If you do badly on a report card or test that you take home on a Friday, you should wait until Sunday night to ask your parents to sign it.

— *Hannah, Age 14*

When you want to stay home from school, you have to stay in the bathroom a long, long time.

— *Joseph, Age 11*

The greatest teacher is not the one who talks all the time, but the one who listens.

— *Lauren, Age 14*

Teach your children a love of reading and you have given them a most precious gift.

Too often we give children answers to remember rather than problems to solve.

— *Roger Lewin*

Of all wild animals, the boy is the most unmanageable.

— *Plato*

When teachers are mad, they don't blink.

— *William, Age 12*

Teachers aren't Einsteins.

— Gabrielle, Age 14

Teachers are the best people in the whole world.

— Natka, Age 14

There is nothing more satisfying than being prepared for a final.

— Jaimee, Age 14

It is better to read the book than the Cliffs Notes.

— Laura, Age 16

Not all learning can be measured by grades.

— Beth, Age 16

**Mary had a little lamb,
Its fleece was white as snow;
And everywhere that Mary went,
The lamb was sure to go.**

**He followed her to school one day;
That was against the rule.
It made the children laugh and play
To see a lamb in school.**

—Sarah Josepha Hale

When a teacher is in a bad mood, there's no way I'm going to ask to go to the bathroom.

— *Angela, Age 11*

If you put a piece of chalk in the blackboard eraser, it drives the teacher crazy!

— *Joshua, Age 8*

If you are in trouble at school, your parents probably already know about it.

— *Rachel, Age 12*

When you don't know what you're doing, ask for help *before* you mess up.

— *Jennifer, Age 14*

You should not mess with the principal.

— Nicholas, Age 9

SCHOOL

Gone is the builder's temple, Crumbled into the dust; Low lies each stately pillar, Food for consuming rust, But the temple the teacher builded Will last while the ages roll, For that beautiful unseen temple Was a child's immortal soul.

— *Hattie Vose Hall*

My teachers can always tell when I start on a project the night before it is due.

— *Emily, Age 10*

Typing class would be a lot easier if I had six fingers on each hand.

— *Andrea, Age 17*

If I study and watch TV at the same time, I end up studying the TV.

— *Charlie, Age 16*

Sometimes a teacher who seems to be totally boring at the beginning of the year turns out to be awesome.

— *Robert, Age 10*

Food

ONE OF MY FAVORITE FOOD QUOTES WAS FROM A SEVEN-YEAR-OLD who confessed, "You can't hide a piece of broccoli in a glass of milk."

Oh, the anguish and frustration of parents who, after preparing and serving a delicious meal, are met with the cry, "This is gross! . . . I'm not eating this! . . . This is the yuckiest thing in the world!"

What we have here is more than a ten-year-old's choice of one of the seven food groups. No, this is a matching of wits and a declaration of independence. This is when food is more than nourishment. On a child's plate, it becomes a weapon.

Children are told when to go to bed, when to get up, what to wear, where to sit, what to say, and how to behave. But with food, it's another matter. Here, they control the agenda, and they know it. All they have to do is put a single green pea in their mouths and pretend to gag. Sometimes once will do. If not, they can keep it up until the cows come home. There are no parents on earth who can sit calmly at a table, watch this charade for more than ten seconds, and not declare an immediate cease-fire. "OK, OK," they surrender. "You can try it again some other time."

The child relaxes. The parents relax. And, under the table, the dog relaxes. He doesn't think much of green peas either.

You can't hide mashed potatoes in your hat.

— *Chris, Age 9*

They put certain things in cafeteria food, so I don't eat there anymore.
— *Kristen, Age 9*

Nothing clears your sinuses like a sandwich with a lot of horseradish.
— *Daniel, Age 17*

"Casserole" is just another word for "leftovers."
— *Elise, Age 14*

Moms make better lunches than dads.
— *Emily, Age 10*

You shouldn't put a marshmallow in the microwave.
— *Mary, Age 12*

FOOD

I know a kid who thinks a balanced meal is a Big Mac in both hands.

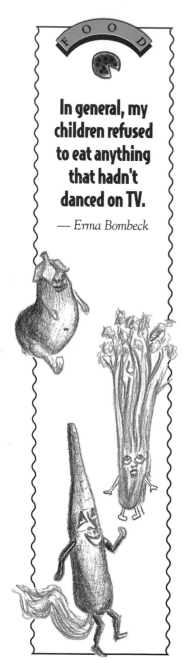

Pizza just isn't the same without extra cheese.

— Elise, Age 14

When food tastes terrible, you can say you have a toothache and you won't have to eat it.

— Nakia, Age 9

You should never try to stick peas in your pocket at dinnertime.

— Renee, Age 13.

You can never be too full for dessert.

— Kelly, Age 10

You should never order seafood at a hamburger joint in Nebraska.

— Chad, Age 11

I can never get away with feeding my broccoli to the dog.

— Joanne, Age 10

A child should always say what's true
And speak when he is spoken to,
And behave mannerly at table;
At least as far as he is able.

— *Robert Louis Stevenson*

You have to do your own growing no matter how tall your grandfather was.

— *Abraham Lincoln*

When you and a friend buy ice cream cones, your friend's flavor always looks better.

— *Amanda, Age 13*

If there is something bad for dinner, your parents don't have to eat it, but you do.

— *Deanna, Age 11*

I am the happiest when I eat won ton soup.

— *Thomas, Age 9*

You can't fake a stomachache right before you're having spinach for dinner.

— *Jessica, Age 11*

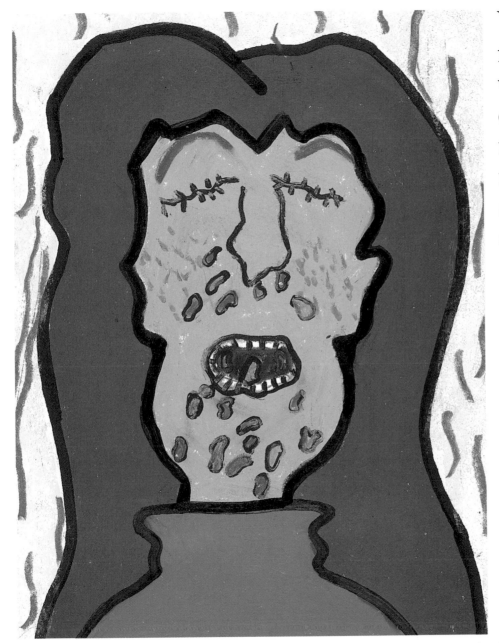

You should never sneeze with a chewed-up nut in your mouth. It's a nasty experience.

— *Amanda, Age 14*

Ask your child what he wants for dinner only if he's buying.

— *Fran Lebowitz*

Children in a family are like flowers in a bouquet; there's always one determined to face in an opposite direction from the way the arranger desires.

— *Anonymous*

I can slurp a slurpie through my nose.

— *Holly, Age 12*

When you are home alone and you eat the chocolate your mom was saving, you should always hide the wrapper and eat a Pop Tart or something so that when your parents get back home, they can't smell your chocolatey breath.

— *David, Age 11*

It's not a very good idea to drink a two-liter Coke before going to bed.

— *Benjamin, Age 15*

School lunches stick to the wall.

— *Patrick, Age 10*

You can't hide a piece of broccoli in a glass of milk.

— *Rosemary, Age 7*

Like a cat, kids enjoy playing with their food before they eat it.

I should never eat my grandma's meatloaf.

— Ron, Age 12

You never eat food after you dissect something in science class. You just might get sick.

— Julie, Age 12

While making cookies, the dough always seems to taste better than the cookie.

— Grace, Age 11

If you put your peas in your mashed potatoes, they don't taste so bad.

— Jonah, Age 10

People will eat things at two o'clock in the morning that they wouldn't eat at any other time.

— Mary, Age 12

Children always need two things: praise and their mouths wiped.

F O O D

A man finds out what is meant by a spitting image when he tries to feed cereal to his infant.

— *Imogene Fey*

Sometimes you take too much food at dinner and you can't eat it. Always make sure you have a baked potato because you can eat the middle and use the skin to hide the food until you take it to the sink. Then shove it down the disposal.

— *Chris, Age 14*

You should never get involved in a good TV show while cooking something in the microwave.

— *Scott, Age 12*

It makes my mommy happy if I keep my mouth closed when I chew my sandwich.

— *Preston, Age 4*

Popping popcorn without a lid isn't smart.

— *Alex, Age 11*

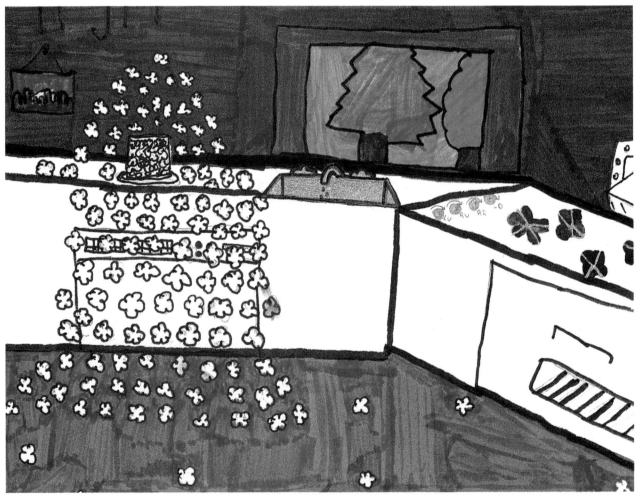

An empty larder is something you come to expect when you live through the locust phase of adolescence.

— *Ellen Goodman*

OUT OF ORDER

You can't trust dogs to watch your food.

— *Patrick, Age 10*

You shouldn't shake a can of pop before opening it.

— *Nicholas, Age 11*

You should never drink anything upside down.

— *Misty, Age 12*

No matter what my mom does to it, spinach always tastes awful.

— *Kelly, Age 11*

Putting your vegetables on your little sister's plate doesn't work.

— *Nicole, Age 11*

There is nothing thirstier than a four-year-old who has just gone to bed.

 I sometimes get a craving for chocolate chip ice cream that cannot be controlled.

— *Rebecca, Age 11*

Meatloaf tastes better after a day in the refrigerator.

— *Bryan, Age 16*

When your mom says, "Try it, you'll like it," you probably won't like it.

— *Emily, Age 10*

When you put a hot dog in the microwave for five minutes, you don't want to be there when your mom sees the mess.

— *Jack, Age 12*

If you want to eat a secret snack, eat it in the basement.

— *Danny, Age 10*

Peanut butter is a food found on bread, kitchen counters, and sofa cushions.

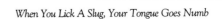

F O O D

My kids can con me into doing things for them by saying, "But it's so much better when you do it, Mom."

—*Muriel J. Trost*

If you don't like what the cafeteria is serving, just put some in your milk carton and you can get away with it.

— *Brandy, Age 12*

I've learned that goldfish don't like jello.

— *Julie Ann, Age 9*

Wise
Beyond Their Years

THE YOUNGSTERS YOU WILL MEET IN THIS CHAPTER demonstrate the genius that most children have for seeing the truth. With innocent hearts and trusting eyes they discover much that is hidden, overlooked, or forgotten by adults.

In his classic book, *The Little Prince*, author Antoine de-Saint Exuprey wrote, "It's only with the heart that we can see rightly." And it's the child's heart, we've learned, that sees clearest of all.

All children are born as sterling silver stars. Our challenge is to prevent society and institutions from beating them into tin cups. Children still shine with a brilliance that comes from minds uncluttered by adult cares and concerns and from youthful spirits free of prejudice and deceit.

Their observations slow us down, turn us around, and cause us to reevaluate our motives and reconsider our future plans. Free of cynicism, these wise words from young hearts prompt us to consider John Greenleaf Whittier's conclusion, "the child must teach the man."

It is time for us adults to take our seats. Our pencils are sharpened and our notebooks open. There is so little time and so much to learn.

You should always listen to older people. They are like living history books and can teach you so much.

— *Cindy, Age 13*

It does not matter how much money a family has. If there is a lot of love in a home, that family is richer than any millionaire could ever be.

— *Whitney, Age 16*

My mom and dad love me no matter what.

— *Abbey, Age 8*

In every child who is born, under no matter what circumstances, and of no matter what parents, the potentiality of the human race is born again.

— *James Agee*

Good habits formed at youth make all the difference.

— *Aristotle*

I should never make a decision unless I'm willing to accept the consequences.

— *Stacy, Age 17*

It's funny how God uses simple people to do great things.

— *Elana, Age 15*

The art of communication is not what you can hear being said from the other person's mouth, but what you can feel from his heart and see in his eyes.

— *Leah, Age 15*

No matter how much you cry at night, things won't change unless you help them to change.

— *Nicole, Age 17*

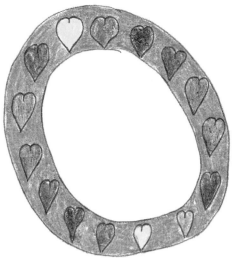

Sometimes the most loving answer is no.

— *Leslie, Age 12*

You should always try, even when you don't think it will help.

— *Jennifer, Age 11*

It is OK to fail, but it is not OK to give up.

— *Kate, Age 8*

W I S E

In short, the habits we form from childhood make no small difference, but rather they make all the difference.

— *Aristotle*

Find something to praise in your child every day.

THE COLOR OF PEOPLE

When You Lick A Slug, Your Tongue Goes Numb

SHOULDN'T MATTER

— Somer, Age 10

A single flower growing where nothing else is growing
is a beautiful thing.

— *Cindy, Age 13*

I should always try my best. If I don't succeed, then at least I will feel good about myself.

— *Laura, Age 16*

Life is hard no matter how old you are.

— *Rosalinda, Age 13*

People are quick to condemn you for the things you've done, but they'll never give you credit for all the times you resisted temptation.

— *Heather, Age 16*

It's never too late to say you're sorry.

— *Laura, Age 12*

The truth is the quickest and easiest way out of trouble.

— *Sarah, Age 12*

Every mother's child is a genius. If you don't believe it, just ask her.

If I were younger, I'd know more.

— *James Barrie*

WISE

Childhood candor... shall I ever find you again?

— *Leo Tolstoy*

Nothing hurts more than guilt.

— Jessica, Age 12

It is a good thing we don't always get what we wish for.

— Rebekah, Age 15

You should be careful around those younger than you. It is surprising how much of an impact a word or action can make on them.

— Sarah, Age 12

A realist is more correct about things in life than an optimist. But the optimist seems to have more friends and much more fun.

— Megan, Age 14

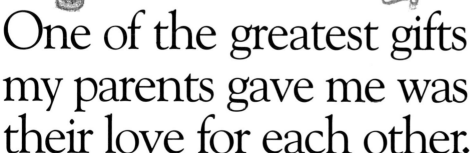

One of the greatest gifts my parents gave me was their love for each other.

— Jamie, Age 16

Children begin by loving their parents; as they grow older, they judge them; sometimes, they forgive them.

— Oscar Wilde

Children have neither past nor future—they rejoice in the present.

Someone is always better than you in one thing, but you are better than them in another.

— *Alecia, Age 12*

Trust is the most valuable thing you'll ever earn.

— *Susanna, Age 17*

You will never be happy if all you do is think about all the things you don't have.

— *Christy, Age 16*

It's good to receive compliments, and it's even better to give them.

— *Aaron, Age 17*

Experience is the Best Teacher

ALL OF US HAVE HAD A GREAT TEACHER at some time. Mine was Miss Mitchell. She was my first-grade teacher, and what I remember best was that she never criticized the colors I used when I drew. "That's lovely," she would say, and my little fingers would eagerly pick up a crayon to draw another purple horse. Partly because of her, I have never been reluctant to take chances.

And then there was Coach Hood who thought I could play first string even though I was twenty pounds lighter than the rest of the squad. In the first game of the season, I ran for two touchdowns. I still carry with me the newfound confidence I felt walking off the field that afternoon. Thank you, Coach Hood.

Then there is the one teacher we all share—the oldest, wisest, and most demanding. When Experience stands at the head of the class, we all pay attention. When is it a good idea not to put on polka-dot underwear? What really happens when you lick a slug? Some lessons cannot be found in books.

We quickly learn that cars roll down steep driveways when the emergency brakes are released and that, nine times out of ten, a tall person will sit in front of a short one at the movies. But sometimes hope triumphs over experience—for there are a few of us who, regardless of how many times we've been disappointed by the picture on the box, still buy the cereal with the toy inside.

EXPERIENCE

Likely as not, the child you can do the least with will do the most to make you proud.

— *Mignon McLaughlin*

Ninty-nine percent of the time things aren't nearly as bad as you first thought they were.

— *Jessica, Age 15*

Piano lessons can make fifteen minutes feel like an hour.

— *Jack, Age 9*

Even though people claim to know what you're going through or dealing with, they don't.

— *Jaimee, Age 14*

What seem to be small gestures of thoughtfulness and kindness can mean a lot—a whole lot.

— *Mary Allyn, Age 17*

If you want something in a cereal box and it looks really big, it always turns out small and crummy.

— *Katie, Age 9*

Every time you get a good seat at the movies, someone taller comes and sits in front of you.

— *Kari, Age 15*

You should never underestimate a child's ability to get into more trouble.

— Ann, Age 15

When you lick a slug, your tongue goes numb.

— Bethany, Age 11

If you give your dog a bath, you get one yourself.

— Mindy, Age 14

I need deodorant.

— Mark, Age 8

No matter how hard you try, you can't baptize cats!

— Laura, Age 13

EXPERIENCE

You have a wonderful child. Then, when he's thirteen, gremlins carry him away and leave in his place a stranger who gives you not a moment's peace.

— Jill Eichenberry

Children need love, especially when they do not deserve it.

— Harold S. Hubert

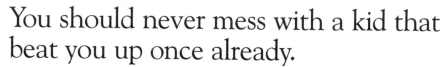

You should never mess with a kid that beat you up once already.

— *Donnie, Age 10*

The key to success is selling my mom's chocolate chip cookies.

— *Rachel, Age 11*

The smaller the print on things, the more important it is.

— *Julie, Age 12*

You shouldn't jump down stairs with your hands in your pockets.

— *Philip, Age 11*

When my dog jumps on my bed, she's going to chase her tail.

— *Jessica, Age 11*

I should never ride my bike in mud when I don't know how deep it is.

— Corey, Age 12

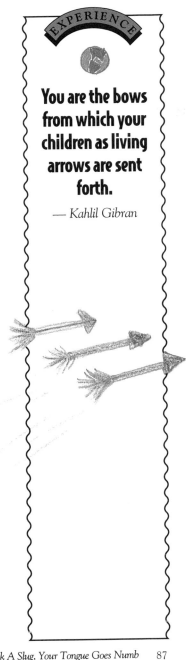
You are the bows from which your children as living arrows are sent forth.

— *Kahlil Gibran*

Children are a great comfort in your old age—and they help you reach it faster, too.

— Lionel Kauffman

My first love was Cinderella, but she ran off with another man.

You'll always get a zit on important days.

— Amanda, Age 14

Some of the most fun I've ever had was after my curfew.

— *Elise, Age 14*

You should never stick a hanger in a light socket.

— *ConiRose, Age 10*

Being late is better than getting a fifty dollar speeding ticket.

— *Laurence, Age 14*

It's not a good idea to spit while on a roller coaster.

— *Scott, Age 11*

Sleeping under the sky and seeing shooting stars is something that you don't want to miss.

— *Melody, Age 14*

EXPERIENCE

When a child enters a room, everything changes.

Never give a child a drum.

You never know how loud you are until you have to be quiet.

— *Sarena, Age 10*

One of the best ways to find out about a person's character is to play Monopoly with them.

— *Ellana, Age 15*

You shouldn't stick your tongue to a car bumper in winter.

— *Tamara, Age 13*

I shouldn't try out my chemistry set on my mom's new dishwasher.

— *Colleen, Age 8*

You should never surprise a cow when you are behind it.

— *Stefanie, Age 12*

My puppy still
has bad breath
even after I gave her
a Tic Tac.

— *Kelly, Age 11*

You never open an umbrella in the car.

— Ryan, Age 7

If you are depressed or upset, just make a list of the things you're upset about and you'll see that the list isn't as long as you thought it was.

— *Heidi, Age 17*

You should never run in a race with your shoelaces untied.

— *Byron, Age 12*

When you get embarrassed and you feel as if everyone is looking at you, no one was looking and they didn't really notice anyway!

— *Alicia, Age 11*

If you sleep in your clothes, you won't have to get dressed in the morning.

— *Stephanie, Age 8 1/2*

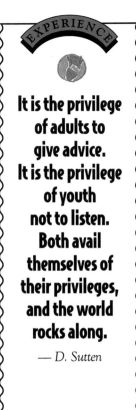

EXPERIENCE

It is the privilege of adults to give advice. It is the privilege of youth not to listen. Both avail themselves of their privileges, and the world rocks along.

— *D. Sutten*

ring ring

Young children step on your feet, older children step on your heart.

— *Old Proverb*

The last day of school before summer vacation is the shortest day of a mother's year.

—*Dee Eldridge*

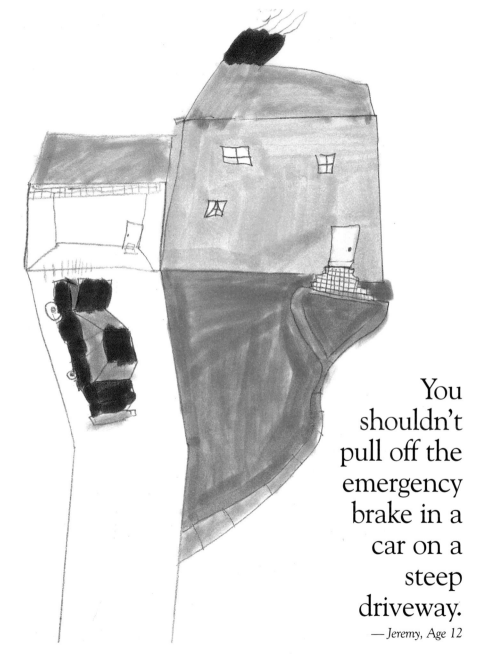

You shouldn't pull off the emergency brake in a car on a steep driveway.

— *Jeremy, Age 12*

If kids are brats when you babysit, don't lie and tell their parents that they were angels because the next time you babysit, they'll be brats again.

— Cassie, Age 15

Every time the family gets a dog and he makes a mess, he suddenly becomes your dog.

— Natalie, Age 13

You shouldn't try and test a nine-volt battery with your braces unless you're looking for an easy way to melt all the rubber bands.

— Chris, Age 14

Life is filled with ups and downs but most of the time I'm going sideways.

— Leslie, Age 11

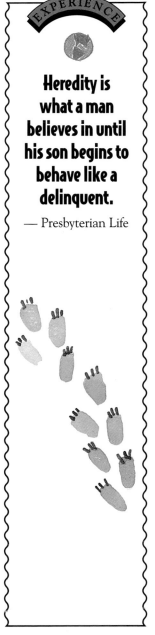

EXPERIENCE

Heredity is what a man believes in until his son begins to behave like a delinquent.

— Presbyterian Life

Youth!
Stay close to the
young and a little
rubs off.

— *Alan Jay Lerner*

Never tell a
young person
that something
cannot be done.
God may have
been waiting
for centuries
for somebody
ignorant
enough of the
impossibility to
do that thing.

— *Dr. J. A. Holmes*

Sitting in the cracks of a couch is more comfortable than sitting in the middle of the cushion.

— *Melody, Age 14*

Seven people in the front seat of a pickup truck just doesn't work.

— *Charlene, Age 16*

Going a little crazy sometimes and doing something out of the ordinary is almost always rewarding.

— *Dawn, Age 14*

If there is anything we wish to change in the child, we should first examine it and see whether it is not something that could better be changed in ourselves.

—Carl Jung

It's dangerous to confuse children with angels.

— David Fyfe

To get me up in the morning, the garbage truck works better than my alarm clock.

— Jessica, Age 10

You shouldn't expect your turtle to come back if you put him in a stream.
— Rosemary, Age 12

Having the ability to play an instrument is priceless.
— Jessica, Age 15

You should never chew on an opened tube of crazy glue.
— Teri, Age 13

You always feel better when you drink peppermint tea and take a hot bath.
— Tammi, Age 15

Don't wear polka-dot underwear under white shorts.
— Jama Lynne, Age 15

It is not a bad thing that children should occasionally, and politely, put parents in their place.

—Colette

There are three ways to get something done: do it yourself, hire someone, or forbid your kids to do it.

— Monta Crane

You shouldn't get attached to a puppy you can't have.

— Jennifer, Age 13

The most dreaded words in the English language are "Some assembly required."

— Grant, Age 9

Moving is one way of getting my room clean.

— Russell, Age 10

It takes more energy to be mad or sad than it does to be happy.

—Jaymin, Age 15

You should never jump out of a tree using trash bags as parachutes.

April, Age 10

You know that the beginning is the most important part of any work, especially in the case of a young and tender thing; for that is the time at which the character is being formed.

— *Plato*

You shouldn't sneeze when someone is cutting your hair.

— Adrienne, Age 12

It isn't worth the effort to wash your dog.

— *Beth, Age 14*

You can't get away with everything, but it's fun to try.

— *Heather, Age 14*

When you buy something with money you've earned, you enjoy it more than when someone else buys it for you.

— *AnnMarie, Age 14*

You should never run around a barn with bare feet.

— *Abbie, Age 15*

When you get a baby out of the tub, put a diaper on it immediately.

— *Jamie, Age 13*

EXPERIENCE

There are only two things a child will share willingly — communicable diseases and his mother's age.

— *Dr. Benjamin Spock*

You should never bite your nails after dissecting a frog.

— *Brooke, Age 17*

You never, ever, ever go to bed with gum in your mouth.

— *Erin, Age 13*

There's a time when you just have to stick your feet out the car window.

— Brooke, Age 17

You don't do pranks at a police station.

— Sam, Age 10

If you give your dad money for gas, you'll never get paid back.

— Shaun, Age 12

You don't use liquid soap in a dishwasher.

— Melinda, Age 13

You can't hide your dog under your bed.

— Bethany, Age 10

EXPERIENCE

The persons hardest to convince they're at the retirement age are children at bedtime.

— Shannon Fife

You should never hold a dustbuster and a cat at the same time.

— Jennifer, Age 15

Even my dog isn't stupid enough to try my sister's cooking.

— John, Age 12

When you lose a pet, it's like losing a best friend.

— Jennifer, Age 9

It hurts a lot to wear rented bowling shoes.

— Paul, Age 11

EXPERIENCE

When I was a boy of fourteen, my father was so ignorant I could hardly stand to have the old man around. But, when I got to be twenty-one, I was astonished at how much he had learned in seven years.

— Mark Twain

It's tough to be a kid, but even tougher to be a good kid.

— *David, Age 9*

Your dog will do tricks for you but not for your friends.

— *Melissa, Age 15*

Cheap goldfish live longer than expensive angelfish.

— *Rebecca, Age 11*

You always think of a good comeback after it's too late.

— *Kim, Age 11*

It's not a good idea to call 911 when there is not an emergency.

— *Corey, Age 7*

Something always goes wrong at weddings.

— Lauren, Age 11

When a girl keeps on teasing you and says she doesn't like you and bugs you all the time, she really likes you.

— Justin, Age 8

No matter how much you think you need it, don't borrow money!

— Amy, Age 12

You can tell what kind of personality a person has by what kind of shoes they wear.

— Brittany, Age 14

You should never tease a goose.

— Robbie, Age 12

There are two things a kid won't stand still for: a face washing and deceiving adults.

There are only two lasting bequests we can hope to give our children. One of these is roots; the other, wings.

— Hodding Carter

My dog sometimes understands me better than my family.

— *Elizabeth, Age 12*

Riding your bike on ice is not as exciting as planning it.

— *Frank, Age 13*

It's hard to say, "I'm sorry," but it's even harder to say, "I forgive you."

— *Heather, Age 12*

If you are going to mix different ingredients in a mixer, don't turn it on high.

— *Victoria Emma Rose, Age 12*

EXPERIENCE

Give a little love to a child, and you get a great deal back.

— *John Ruskin*

Nothing speaks more loudly to a child than a good parent's quiet example.

You shouldn't try to do fifteen cartwheels in a row.

— *Vanessa, Age 10*

You should never jump off your top bunk and expect to fly.

— *Becky, Age 8*

If you have a study date with a guy you like, nine out of ten times you won't get any studying done.

— *Kathryn, Age 16*

If you keep the class pet hamster, it's bound to get away.

— *Keely, Age 10*

Priceless

"Come in, come in. There's something I want to show you."
An old friend had dropped by my office as I was making the final selection of quotes and artwork for this book. First, I described to her the concept and then read my favorite entries from this chapter. I mentioned that "Priceless" seemed to be an appropriate title because every time I read the entries, I would think, "That's priceless." No other response seemed appropriate.

"What a coincidence," she said, and began to tell me this story. Several months before, she had been going through her late father's papers and found some letters written to him by her grandmother. The time was after World War II and her father was still in the army and a long way from home. In the dusty, old envelopes, attached to the letters, were slips of paper on which her grandmother had recorded things my friend had said when she was four years old. And, next to each of the pearls of wisdom, her grandmother had added her own comment, "Priceless." "Now, I was no smarter than the average four-year-old," she admitted, "but I was flattered that my family would find my youthful comments so intriguing."

That's the magic and mystery of children's observations. They surprise us with their sensitivity and inspire us with their insight. And perhaps most important of all, they challenge us to consider the things that make life really worth living.

No matter how old you are, you always think that there may be something hiding under the bed.

— *Monica, Age 13*

Lying drives your conscience crazy.

— *Kyle, Age 10*

Dogs and mothers will love you no matter what.

— *Heather, Age 16*

Simply saying, "I believe in you" can make someone's day.

— *Mary, Age 16*

If you want to make your parents feel good, write them a small note before you go to bed saying, "I love you."

— *Kari, Age 11*

No one notices what I do until I don't do it.

— Lorie, Age 14

A pen and paper are all you need to create a new world.

— Michelle, Age 13

You can't always be the best, but you should always try your best.

— Jeannie, Age 13

There are not too many things you can do in life, good or bad, that someone else doesn't find out about.

— Leia, Age 16

It's better to look back and say "at least I tried," than look back and say "if only."

— Margo, Age 17

Pretty much all the honest truth telling there is in the world today is done by children.

— *Oliver Wendell Holmes*

When you pray, you get a happy feeling inside like God just walked into your heart and is warming himself at a cozy fire.

— *Charles, Age 16*

The best place to go with a child is in their imagination.

— *Amie, Age 16*

If you believe in yourself, anything is possible.

— *Meghann, Age 13*

Today is one of a kind and will only happen once—so make it great!

— *Donna, Age 17*

The world is a wonderful place and everyone should shut up and enjoy it every once in a while.

— *Sarah, Age 12*

You're never too old for a teddy bear.

— Katie, Age 11

Youth is wholly experimental.

— *Robert Louis Stevenson*

Every child is an artist. The problem is how to remain an artist once he grows up.

— *Pablo Picasso*

The best place to be when you are sad is in your grandma's lap.

— *Jeannie, Age 7*

You can't change the past, but you have choices for the future.

— *Jaymin, Age 15*

You should never let your fears become the boundaries of your dreams.

— *Robin, Age 15*

The more mistakes I make, the smarter I get.

— *Jennifer, Age 13*

Someone always needs help.

— *Sarah, Age 10*

Childhood is not preparation for life. It is life.

— *James, Age 9*

A community's greatest investment is that which it has in its youth. It cannot do too much to develop healthy sports, good schools, and libraries. They all pay dividends in good citizenship.

— *George Matthew Adams*

In all the countries I've been to, everyone understands a smile.

— *Jennifer, Age 14*

I should be patient with the annoying; the most questioning child could open a new door.

— *Michelle, Age 13*

I like to draw because it makes my mind flow.

— *Todd, Age 10*

If you are quiet, you may hear a compliment.

— *Kristy, Age 12*

"Guests" is just another word for "cleaning."

— *Chanelle, Age 12*

In a difficult situation, my parents need me to be strong, because that makes them strong.

— *Kathryn, Age 16*

PRICELESS

You are as young as your faith, as old as your doubt; as young as your self-confidence, as old as your fear; as young as your hope, as old as your despair. In the central place of every heart, there is a recording chamber; so long as it receives messages of beauty, hope, cheer and courage, so long are you young.

— *Gen. Douglas MacArthur*

Smiles are wondrous things; you can give them out for eternity and always have one left for yourself.

— Colleen, Age 13

You always have time for someone you care for.

— Lois, Age 11

You can't push away your conscience.

— Christopher, Age 12

There are few things that country music, honesty, time, ice cream, forgiveness, or a hug won't heal.

— Heather, Age 16

You can travel inside a book.

— Jameson, Age 8

Acknowledgments

I would like to thank the following contributors for their insights and observations: Rebekah Abel, Julie Akerson, Becky Allen, Katie M. Allen, Chad Almy, Todd Douglas Amundsen, Alecia Anderson, Kara Anderson, Alex Arnett, Laura Balshuweit, Sam Bartholomew, Jaymin Beck, William Beins, Charlene Bellemore, Amy Benedetto, Robin Benway, Kellie Bethke, Kim Bieke, Natka Bianchini, Eddie Bishop, Stacy Bissonette, Joanne Bozue, Beth Brennenstuhl, Melissa Brewer, Rosemary Brown, Sarah Brown, Sean Browne, Mary Allyn C. Buyco, Jamie Campbell, Donna Cappello, Mary Carpenter, Jaimee Case, Christopher Cassella, Nicholas D. Castle, Frank Chen, Philip Christenson, Misty Clough, Laura Cohen, Angela Collins, Melissa Colon, Jennifer Costello, Elizabeth Cowley, Holly Cravath, Abbie Croft, Bryan Davis, Vanessa De La Rosa, Tiffany Deines, Ellana Delaney, Ashley Dinney, Katherine Dmochowski, Julie Anne Dous, Lindsay Drake, Natalie M. Drake, Brittany Dunning, David N. Duquette, Nakia Eggerson, Kyle T. Emmons, Keely Emrick, Matthew Engelkes, Emily Ericksen, Kari Evans, Chris Farquhar, Brian Fattorini, Morgan Faulk, Andrea Ferry, Dawn Finley, Rosalinda Flores, Leah Fortenberry, Victoria Emma Rose Foster, Patrick Fraunfelder, Jessica Frey, Byron Friedrichsen, ConiRose Fusco, Rosemary Futrell, David Gallichio, Emily Gary, Abbey Ghegan, Megan Gillespie, Danny Giuditta, Stepfanie Gowen, Gabrielle Gramazio, Jennifer Lee Grant, Erin Grass, Lindsay Ellen Greene, Rebecca Greenstein, Reza Grigorian, Katie Grim, Melinda Groff, Mary R. Gross, Maria Guelig, Tiffany A. Hall, Heather Hamilton, Kathryn Hamilton, Laura Harbert, Jeffrey Harrington, Cindy Hatcher, Jennifer Hatcher, Lorie Hayden, Beth Headrick, Kelly Herrmann, Carrie Herzog, Rebecca Hester, Lauren Hickmon, Amanda Hightower, Nichole Hill, Mark Hines, Abby Holmes, Angela Horner, Russell Hudson, Leslie S. Hughes, Lauren Jobe, Tammi Johnson, Amanda L. Karioth, Rachel Kassel, Chris Keeney, Teri Kern, Charlie King, Andrea Kolski, Erin Kossoris, Kari Kraemer, Benjamin Laird, Michelle Lambiasi, Joseph J. LaTorre II, Christie Lazzara, Kristy Lee, Melody Lee, Aaron J. Lenhart, Nicole Lichty, Chanelle Loftness, Shaun Luebbe, Sarena Luke, Cory Mace, Corey Macha, Renee Marks, Nicholas John Marrone, Michael Mattingly, Corey McAtee, Sarah McClain, John McRoberts, Katie McWeeney, Jeannie Miles, Joel Miller, Jeremy Mills, April Mirvis, Lindsey Lauren Moore, Kim Mull, AnnMarie Murphy, Jennifer S. Murray, Jameson Murphy Muth, Deanna Needell, Julie Nelson, Amie Newsome, Adrienne Nichols, Emily Nixon, Neely North, Donnie O'Neill, Brooke Pace, Cassie Parks, Ann Pate, Erin Pearson, Jessica Penney, Matthew Pernat, Grace Peterson, Preston Phelan, Joseph Phillips, Kate K. Phillips, Julie Ann Poling, Heather Poplin, John Potesta, Susanna Poulson, Amber Powell, Kelly Ralabate, Jessica P. Read, Leslie Rector, Robbie Roberts, Joseph D. Robinette, Kristen Rodner, Jennifer Ann Roper, Jessica Ross, Shanna M. Ross, Laura Salmon, Jessica Ah Sam, Emily Ann Sander, Jonah Saving, Rachel Schryer, Jennifer Scott, Elizabeth Scruggs, Justin Seibel, Nicholas Selan, Elise Selinger, Colleen Shaw, Hannah Shearer, Meghann Shutt, Amanda Sloane, Megan Smith, Tina Smith, Adam Solzsmon, Jessica Southern, David Speer, Stefanie Sperry, Devin Spinks, Scott Sprague, Mindy Sprouse, Leslie Starnes, Colleen Steg, Brandy Stenson, Samuel Stern, Angela Stevens, Charles L. Stewart, Elana Stewart, Jama Lynne Stinnett, Katie Stolowitz, Robert Strube, Thomas Strube, Joanna Stubblebine, Daniel Summers, Ryan Sweet, Calen Swift, Julie Taylor, Wendy Taylor, Brian Thompson, Chase Thompson, Matt Thorson, Bethany Throw, Monica Tiu, Scott D. Tompkins, Alicia Trider, Melissa Turner, Tamara Ulmer, Laurence Van Atten, Bethany D. Vermaas, Christopher Viney, Grant Voyles, Elizabeth Carrison Waite, Whitney Wallace, Jeannie Waller, Somer Weber, Lezlee Wheeler, Joshua White, Jessica R. Williams, Jennifer Wintas, Sarah Wolfe, Stephanie Wood, Heather Wrigley, Christy Wuenstel, James Zetlin, Jamie Ziegler, and Jill Zupancic.

I am also grateful to those children whose art work was submitted for the book including: Susan Adams, Libby Andress, Julie Andress, Jenny Aranson, Lainey Bornstein, Kim Boyle, Freddy Brown, Scott Caven, Miriam Clay, Ellen Cohen, Kasey Coleman, Chris Cox, Kate Cunningham, Anika Dharamrup, Laura Donnelly, Stephen Drummond, Joshua Duke, Colt Duncan, Cherish Duran, Charlie Dykstra, Taryn Edward, Shawn Marie Evans, LaTerra Everhart, Rachel Fox, Tiffany Gourley, Amanda Graham, Benjamin Gude, Lindsay Handelsman, Kiri Hassan, Leon Hathaway, William Hayslett, Angie Hickerson, Dennis Hume, Jasmin Jata, Chris Jayne, Burkitt Jensen, Kareem Khoury, Kimberly Kincaid, Kate W. Lainhart, Zac Lane, Carolyn Long, Margaret, Daniel Marker-Moore, Mary Beth Marley, Margaret McDermott, Katherine Moore, Jane Mosbacher, Steven Myers, Katie Overhold, Mary Kathryn Paynter, Avery Lynn Pickard, Sara Pilzer, Jessica Reguli, Brad Reinhardt, Kenny Richardson, Navit Robkin, Natasha Samoylenka, Michael Schneider, Laura Sensenig, Stuart Shapiro, Laura Siegfried, Andrea Siskin, Carrie Smith, Ali Spizman, Amanda Taggart, Chase Thompson, Lacey Thompson, Enbard Toledano, Stephanie Wesolowski, B.J. Wiser, Courtney Wrenn.

Finally, there were a number of teachers who inspired their students to provide art for the book. Without their help, this project would not have been possible: Harriet Kinslow and Dr. Jean Litterer, Hillsboro High School; Harriet Renner and Grace Good, Rice Elementary; Judy Smith, Lincoln School; Margaret Madden, Jan Anderson, and Cindy Davis, Phoenix Country Day School; Cheryl Finkel, Epstein School; Janice Hughes, The Galloway School; Elizabeth Cohen, Greenfield Hebrew Academy; Amanda Dunn, Heards Elementary; Freddie Williams and Heidi Wallace, Rebecca Minor Elementary; Judy Smith, Lincoln School; Suzanne Hemleben, Hattie Casey Elementary; Joyce Applegate, Cincinnati Country Day School; Mary Ann Gemmill, Goodlettsville Elementary School; Janet Brown, McGavock Elementary School; Nancy Joplin, Housman Elementary School; Linda Woods, St. John's School; Karen Rainey and Carol Swaim, Hubbard Middle School; Robyn Spizman; Brenda Laird; Barry McAllister; Claudia Duke; John Guider; Bill Jayne; Teena Thompson; and Melissa Gray. And a special thanks to my niece, Hollye Schumacher for her assistance.

An Invitation

I invite youngsters, ages five to sixteen, to write to me and to share their wit and wisdom in case I should decide to put together a second collection. I would also be delighted to receive artwork illustrating your observations. The size of the artwork should not exceed 8-1/2 x 11 inches, and any technique or medium is acceptable. Regrettably, the artwork cannot be returned. My address is:

H. Jackson Brown, Jr.
P. O. Box 150285
Nashville, Tennessee 37215